The Heartbeat of
Anguish!

The Pain of Birthing
the Dreams of God

by David Mayorga

SHABAR PUBLICATIONS
www.shabarpublications.com

Most Shabar Publications products are available at special quantity discounts for bulk purchase for sales promotions, fund-raising and educational needs. For details, write Shabar Publications at mayorga1126@gmail.com.

The Heartbeat of Anguish! *The Pain of Birthing the Dreams of God* by David Mayorga

Published by Shabar Publications
3833 N. Taylor Rd.
Palmhurst, Texas 78573
www.shabarpublications.com

Unless otherwise noted, all Scripture quotations are from the New Kings James Version of the Bible. Copyright@1979, 1980, 1982 by Thomas Nelson, Inc., publishers. Used by permission.

Cover of this Book. I want to thank David Ravenhill for the inspiration and sharing his creativity with me in developing the concept that birthed the idea for the cover of this book.

Note: This publication contains the opinions and ideas of its author(s). It is intended to provide helpful and informative material on the subject matter covered. It is sold with the understanding that the author(s) and publisher are not engaged in rendering professional service in the book. If the reader requires personal assistance or advice, a competent professional should be consulted. The author(s) and publisher specifically disclaim any responsibility for any liability, loss, or risk, personal or otherwise, which is incurred as a consequence, directly or indirectly, of the use and application of any of the contents of this book.

Table of Content

Dedication

I want to dedicate this book to the many who have caught a glimpse of God's dream or vision and have labored for it to come to pass.

It wasn't easy; it didn't come naturally, and it took every ounce of your strength to see it manifest.

In all your waiting and praying and then more waiting, God taught you to be patient while working deep within your heart. When the last tear was shed, and the last cry was made, God broke through with a glorious revelation of Himself- not before but after the brokenness.

It was then, and could have been only then, that the anguish was lifted!

To all who waited and pleaded with God for countless hours, days, weeks, months, and even years in prayers and fasting, in much loneliness and anguish to see the manifestation of God's heart ... I bless you!

This book is the testimony of Hannah, Samuel's mother. May we be discipled and mentored by this great woman of God, who, though dead, still speaks!

-David Mayorga, *Author*

Foreword

"Give me children, or else I die." This was the cry of a barren woman's deep desperation, frustration, rejection, and emotional pain.

She is surrounded by all her sister's children, who also happen to be her husband's other wife and rival.

She was daily reminded of her own barren state of feeling forgotten and hopeless, which eventually caused even her husband to lash out at her as though he could change her painful plight.

Her name, as you recall, was Rachel, the mother of Joseph.

It's one thing to endure a short season of emotional pain but another thing entirely for the pain to last for years on end.

You may be surprised that some of God's greatest servants can be traced back to barren women. Hannah, who many believe was Elkanah's first wife, was replaced due to her bareness by Elkanah's second wife, Peninnah. Hannah's womb had been closed by God Himself but was miraculously opened, allowing her to give birth to no other than Samuel, one of Israel's greatest prophets. Then we have Manoah who became the mother of Samson. She also was barren until God touched her.

In the New Testament, we have Elizabeth, the mother of none other than John the Baptist, the forerunner of Jesus. God opened her womb long after she was capable in the natural of having children.

Jesus began His greatest teaching with these words. **"Blessed are the poor in spirit, for theirs is the kingdom of heaven."**

The word poor is more literally translated as beggar. A beggar is someone who has come to the end of his own resources and ability and can only survive by begging or living from someone else's resources.

A barren woman, in many ways, is like a beggar. She no doubt has tried to conceive only to find out or be told that she is incapable of bearing children of her own.

One can only imagine the emotional heartache of seeing friends and neighbors with families of their own and yet unable to be a parent yourself. Emotions would lead to questions like, why me?

This, in turn, would lead to feeling rejected, useless, and without hope.

For the married woman, the pain would no doubt cause her to feel useless as well as feeling guilty about robbing her husband of being a father or having a family of his own.

While all the above may be true in the natural it can also be true spiritually.

Perhaps you have held a dream in your heart or clung to some promise only to watch the years go by while the promise remains as elusive as ever.

Spiritual bareness can lead to either discouragement and despair or determination—the determination not to copy someone else's ministry but to press into God as never before. Remember His word through Isaiah in chapter 54:1: **"Shout for joy, O barren one, you who have born no child; break forth into shouting and cry aloud, you who have not travailed. For the sons of the desolate one will be more numerous than the sons of the married woman."**

For over twenty years, I've carried in my bible a small photocopy of a Lufthansa ad. Lufthansa is Germany's number-one airline carrier. The ad wording, less than three inches by two, was positioned in the lower portion of the first page of a *Time* magazine. The rest of the page showed a plane taking off at sunrise. Here is exactly how the ad appeared:

At Lufthansa, we believe a well-trained pilot is the most import-ant safety device there is. So important, that we built our own flight schools in Bremen, Germany and Phoenix, Arizona, just so our pilots are trained to the highest standards. But even before they can go through our rigorous program, they first have to get in. Each year we recruit 6,000 applicants to undergo tough psychological and intelligence testing. Only about 340 pass. And from there, it takes around 19 year's experience to finally become a captain on a Boeing 747. So, you know your smooth flight on Lufthansa is no coincidence. It's the result of a passion, not to mention years and years of preparation.

I keep what is now a rather worn copy of this ad in my bible to remind myself that if a secular airline takes that much time to secure the safety of its passengers, not to mention the compa-ny's own reputation. How much more is God concerned about the well-being of His precious children and His own reputa-tion?

God is never in a hurry when preparing vessels for His purposes. Jesus himself was thirty years old before he began his ministry. Moses was forty years on the backside of the desert in preparation for his leadership role. Joseph was imprisoned as part of his training. I believe the greater the calling, the longer the preparation.

All too many individuals who dreamed of God's high calling failed because they were not prepared to wait for God's timing, submit to God's training, or allow Him to purify their motives.

If spiritual barrenness describes your life, this book is for you.

My good friend David Mayorga delves into Hannah's story and uncovers timeless principles that provide hope and instruction for all who have all but given up on ever being used by God.

I believe the reason Hannah had to wait so long was that God was waiting to hear these words: **"O Lord of hosts, if Thou wilt indeed look on the affliction of Thy maidservant and remember me, and not forget Thy maidservant, but will give Thy maidservant a son, then I will give him to the Lord all the days of his life..."**

Now that her motives were pure, God could entrust her with the birth of one of Israel's great prophets, Samuel.

Take this book with you into the closet (of prayer) and ask the Lord to teach you, His ways. I know He will.

-David Ravenhill, *Author, and Itinerant Teacher*
Siloam Springs, Arkansas

Introduction

In my experience of living and walking with God, I have watched people of vision for the last 35-plus years and have noticed that they are a bit different from your common servant-leader, who might be content with simply carrying out spiritual exercises, attending their local congregations, and helping here and there when able.

Some live as if everything around them is fine and feel no burden for the world around them. They have no fire burning deep within for the heart of God; they have not experienced the revelation that out of his heart will flow rivers of living water, as Jesus said in John 7:38.

The type of servant who has caught a glimpse of the life to come lives very differently, almost as if they are in tune or rhythm to the beat of a different drummer. These servants of God are the faith-led servants who have established divine order on the earth, and their passion shows it.

Their demeanor is also different. They continue to live challenging lives and fight for the right way to live. They are not content with their generation's status quo; God has touched them, and their tears show it.

For some reason, the Apostle Paul comes to mind when he said in Galatians 6:17: **"...for I bear on my body the** [brand] **marks of the Lord Jesus** [the wounds, scars, and other outward evidence of persecutions—these testify to His ownership of me]**!"** The type of servant I'm referring to here has allowed God to brand them and make them all His. They have all over their lives the branding (spiritual and natural) marks of the Lord Jesus and will only rest until they take hold of what has taken hold of them.

Hannah's life is an example of such a vessel. Get ready to be challenged by this woman of God as she teaches us the heartbeat of anguish—the pain of giving birth to God's dreams.

Chapter 1

All I Wanted Were Children?

"...but Hannah had no children..." (1 Samuel 1:2)

In reading the story of Hannah in 1 Samuel chapter 1, little did I know that the Lord would reveal to my heart this incredible revelation regarding vision and purpose for the future.

About twenty years ago, I received this fresh word as I crossed challenges in my life and ministry. It could not have come any sooner, but God knew what He would reveal to me would impact my life profoundly.

While I meditated upon the life of Hannah, Elkanah's wife, it quickly registered that this story was not only about a young wife desiring children or her inability to have any due to barrenness.

I quickly discovered that the Holy Spirit wanted to use this specific story to teach me more about the human heart's longing and how God deposits things in it and stirs us to reach for them.

It was a story about God's passion, desire, and ability to give birth to dreams that only He could bring to pass. It was a story about perseverance in prayer and keeping the faith until the manifestation comes.

Hannah vs. Peninnah

There is not much regarding Hannah's life. It says she married Elkanah, who also had another wife called Peninnah. Peninnah had children, but Hannah did not and could not.

Now, I don't think, or at least I don't believe, that Hannah knew she was barren, and neither did her husband know until much later. I mean, how could she know?

It is my natural thinking that Hannah aspired to start a family like any young wife. Her aspirations of being a godly mother one day were on the agenda, and the possibilities of teaching her children the ways of Jehovah God were genuine.

Everything seemed to be in place, and she was now waiting for her impregnation. But time after time, day after day, nothing happened.

From Hannah's perspective, life was great, so it seemed, until...

She could not come out pregnant, yet Peninnah could.

This whole situation began a revolution of thoughts in her. Things began to change for Hannah when Peninnah started to provoke or make fun of her. These gestures produced many negative emotions and thoughts.

Only someone who has experienced barrenness can truly understand the heart of Hannah. Only someone with this type of longing can sympathize with this dear servant of the Lord named Hannah.

It Takes Someone!

In the silence of Hannah's life, she had to have been pondering this abnormality of not having children. Maybe she blamed her husband, maybe she blamed herself, or perhaps she felt God was to be blamed for this barrenness.

You see, our lives can be at a standstill for weeks, months, or even years until God sends someone to stir us up, someone to provoke us to the point of breaking.

Many of us have dreams and desires that God has given us, but we have put them to rest since they have never manifested. At the same time, God sends people our way to provoke those dreams in us to life! Have you had this happen to you lately? If you need more time, get ready!

It may come through various sources: a job, an opportunity, a friend, an acquaintance, a coworker, or even a family member.

I am going back to Hannah's testimony . . .

Can you imagine the feeling of not being able to bring children into the world; how about the overwhelming thoughts of uselessness, not to mention the feeling of rejection and reproach brought upon her by her inability to bear children?

The feeling of failure is just a little behind. She felt like a failure while looking in the mirror, before her husband Elkanah, and in the presence of family and friends. You get the picture!

But how did she know that she was barren? How did Hannah know that life would be like this? She didn't ask for this! Yet, Hannah found herself in an impossible situation. I can think of many situations filled with difficulty and adversity from within and from without.

An Impossible Situation!

As God's servants, we are often placed in such a situation. We know that God created us for Him and to manifest His glory to the world, but we fall short of doing anything He desires from us.

The desire and passion to be or do something for the glory of God are ever-present deep within, but we can't find the power to carry it out. We feel unable, unskilled, and unprepared; we see every opportunity as impossible and unreachable.

Many of us have been here at this very place; some of you reading this book are now experiencing this in your own life. The fact that you are reading this book reflects the anguish in your heart for a significant breakthrough! You know it, I know it, and even better, God knows it!

As a side note, God knows your desires because He is the One who placed them deep inside you. God is not surprised by the things you carry in your spiritual womb – He put them there! Did you know that?

Too often, it is hard to express a spiritual pregnancy to people. Though people know that God speaks to the human spirit and impregnates it with vision, purpose, and desire, too many believers are clueless as to this form of belief. They don't have a single clue that the Lord desires to birth something out of your spiritual womb. It is something that will bring Him glory and will provide a solution to many.

Never discard the deep emotions that God places deep inside of you. Please don't take them lightly. I believe the Lord places concepts, ideas, and strategies and uses us as vehicles to bring them forth.

Remember, these feelings must be God-birthed. I'm not saying that every emotion is Spirit-led. Some are not Spirit-led but fleshly-led. One must discern the difference.

Chapter 2

Hannah's Internal & External Rivals

"And her rival also provoked her severely, to make her miserable, because the LORD had closed her womb." (1 Samuel 1:6)

In reading Hannah's story and her barrenness issue, I can imagine the deep introspection she would do when she was alone. How do I know this? Because I have done it, yes, I have had to make many introspections in my own life about so many matters. You have done the same.

While Hannah lived her life daily, whether in the morning or late afternoon, she could hear the children crying. Oh, but wait! It wasn't her children; they were Peninnah's kids.

Self-Pity Avenue

Sometimes, we look at other people's successes and wonder why our lives are unsuccessful. At least from where we stand, we can see how God has blessed others in many ways! A sinking feeling comes upon us, and we start to feel sorry for ourselves. How many times have you visited Self-Pity Avenue?

The feeling that God chose to bless others and not you must be one of the devil's deadliest weapons in his arsenal against God's servants. Nothing discourages a man or woman of God like the feeling of unproductivity.

Resting on your call and responsibility should be enough to encourage you in your walk with God, but it is not pleasing to the flesh! The flesh screams, "It's unfair, it's unjust, it's favoritism, etc."

According to Your Ability!

Some months back, I heard a podcast of a particular servant of God being interviewed. The man talked about how God had used all these servants significantly. All through history, God had raised people to make a difference all around the world, and on and on, he added.

As I continued hearing him speak, something gripped my heart, and I knew it wasn't God, and it wasn't good! This deep churning in my gut and this wicked whisper became more intense in me, saying, "You are a loser; you will never amount to anything; you will never produce to your capacity; you are cursed and will never succeed!"

At the end of the podcast, the man promoted his book on the subject he was sharing.

Listen to my honest thoughts and hear what I said to myself: I'm interested in this subject. If I read this book, I will become a superhero like him. I will read it carefully, study his principles, and be like him – successful and relevant. It sounds funny now, but that was my state of mind when I heard this man. By the way, I did order the book. It's collecting dust in my library.

When I got the book, I began reading it. It was an excellent book. It was so good that I called a friend of mine, David Ravenhill, and told him all about it. I consider David Ravenhill one of this generation's most balanced men of God.

Without knowing, David ministered to me. He didn't see the battle I was in but very calmly proceeded to share God's heart with me. David Ravenhill told me, "David, God gave people talents according to their ability. We are called to be faithful with what God gave us." I started feeling those chains breaking off me. My friend David had no idea.

God Will Reward You Accordingly

Then he shared a bit from this story: **"For the kingdom of** heaven is like a landowner who went out early in the morning to hire laborers for his vineyard. Now when he had agreed with the laborers for a denarius a day, he sent them into his vineyard. And he went out about the third hour and saw others standing idle in the marketplace, and said to them, 'You also go into the vineyard, and whatever is right I will give you.' So they went. Again, he went out about the sixth and the ninth hour, and did likewise. And about the eleventh hour he went out and found others standing idle, and said to them, 'Why have you been standing here idle all day?' They said to him, 'Because no one hired us.' He said to them, 'You also go into the vineyard, and whatever is right you will receive.' "So, when evening had come, the owner of the vineyard said to his steward, 'Call the laborers and give them their wages, beginning with the last to the first.' And when those came who were hired about the eleventh hour, they each received a denarius. But when the first came, they supposed that they would receive more; they likewise received each a denarius." (Matthew 20:1-10)

Not only does God call us to serve Him, but He also rewards us accordingly. We must always have this before us and rest upon God's wisdom. The servant of God must rest on these facts of Scripture.

If the flesh is not kept in check, the temptation to feel less, unappreciated, unwanted, or unnecessary will creep in.

I'll forever thank God for David Ravenhill and the nuggets of wisdom he provided to help me navigate this particular season.

Beware of Jealousy & Envy!

It is one thing to feel sorry for yourself and feel like a failure for not being more productive, but I dare say that nothing is worse than being possessed by envy and jealousy.

What is Envy?

The definition for **envy**, according to Wikipedia, *is an emotion that occurs when a person lacks another's quality, skill, achievement, or possession and wishes that the other lacked it.*

Can you see this happening to Hannah? Can you see this happening to you? It's an emotion that occurs when others have what you want. How many of you have been to this place in your life?

What is Jealousy?

The definition of **jealousy** is like envy but a little different. *Jealousy generally refers to the thoughts or feelings of insecurity, fear, and concern over a relative lack of possessions or safety.*

These two words seem synonymous; nonetheless, they relate to what you feel [as an emotion] when others have or possess something you don't.

This was one of Hannah's most significant battles in her journey. I am sure other emotions played a role in her life, but these two must have been present.

Vicious Peninnah

Apart from the internal battles that Hannah was challenged with, we still have one more to attend to, one more rival named Peninnah.

As if anger, envy, and jealousy weren't enough, she had to deal with the other woman named Peninnah. The Scripture says that this woman would "provoke her severely, to make her miserable."

What seems interesting to me is how this woman Peninnah had no heart of compassion for this barren woman. She had no mercy and beat Hannah with all her might. She tortured her emotionally, and one would think what a wicked person Peninnah is!

Some questions come to my mind as we move on to the next chapter.

Would God allow Peninnah to provoke Hannah to the point of making her miserable? If He allowed it, then why would He? Then again, why would He not? If God is preparing His vessel to give birth to something, wouldn't He do all He can to make it come to pass? Ponder this as we continue this journey.

Chapter 3

Barrenness!

"...because the LORD had closed her womb." (1 Samuel 1:6b)

What is barrenness? How is this word defined? Let's look at it. Several dictionaries have barrenness defined as 1) the quality of yielding nothing of value and 2) the state (usually of a woman) of having no children or being unable to have children.

In pondering these definitions, I can see how they affect the person. For example, when a woman cannot have children naturally, her spirit and soul can be broken at the thought of yielding nothing of value. Do you see this?

I believe that this was the case in Hannah's life. She was overwhelmed by her inability to have children. I don't know if she spends long hours talking to the neighbor and, in a roundabout way, shares her pain. I mean, what do you do when you face such a situation?

You see, in those days, for a woman to be barren was nothing more than a sign of some type of curse upon her life. If that wasn't hard enough, she also had Peninnah, the other wife. That was Elkanah's other wife. This woman was Hannah's number one rival, no doubt; she would provoke her severely!

What do you suppose that Hannah did with this inward battle? Did she hide from everyone so that she didn't have to give any explanations? Perhaps she blamed the people around her for this embarrassing season in her life.

No matter how she felt, her situation was as actual as it gets, and I believe she needed more than people understanding her. I am very thankful for the friends that have gathered around me when in duress; God knows I am very grateful for sincere servants of God who want to lend a hand, yet their help always seems to be limited – for the matter at hand has to do with spiritual depth, yes, the deep spiritual marrow of our bone!

Did Anyone Care?

I have often thought that people who have ailments or those who are hurting deep inside usually hurt alone. I have seen this, and I have experienced this.

I have seen people hurt alone in the dark with no one around to bring a soothing word of comfort or offer help in some small way. I am sure we have all experienced this to some degree.

Does it matter if anyone can supply help or offer encouragement? Some people will say yes, it is a good thing, while others may think and say it doesn't make a difference. Perhaps, in some ways, it brings comfort, but I venture to say that in the big scheme of things, natural help can't help a spiritual need.

I can picture people surrounding Hannah and showering her with words of comfort, gifts, cards, flowers, and prayers done on her behalf, only for her to say thank you but leave it unchanged! Instead of celebrating birthdays, they became nothing more than a reminder that she was running out of time to have children! Do you hear me?

Sometimes, people make going through a rough patch in life a lot easier, but it doesn't take away the pain.

When my 101-year-old mother passed away, people surrounded me, embraced me, and gave kind words of sympathy, and that was very nice. Still, truth be told, once everyone left, I was left with loneliness and the absence of my mother never coming back to her bedroom ever again. I don't mean to sound insensitive, but this is also part of the life cycle, and I repeat, *we can't take away a spiritual problem with natural means.*

Hannah's battle had just begun, and it would be like no other she had ever experienced. She would have to fight a different battle, an epic spiritual battle, on behalf of the generations to come. You see, no one knew that; only her empty womb could feel the depth of this pain.

The Race Is On!

As I have attempted to define barrenness, perhaps you are going through some of this barrenness. Perhaps barrenness just like Hannah; perhaps barrenness at work, in your vocation, in your family, in your ministry, in your future projects, in your relationships, etc.

You feel something should be happening, but it isn't. You try to move forward only to end up where you started. You are racing against people's comments and criticisms, fighting against negative thoughts of despair and disappointment, and yes, racing against the clock of life that reminds you daily that you are not getting any younger! You try, but nothing is being conceived; nothing is being birthed!

Lonely Nights and Days!

I know some people who face depression, maybe not daily, but they have had their bouts with it. I have seen people deal with it and have overcome this struggle, but I also have seen others succumb to this horrible experience of anxiety and depression. It is not a good time in that person's life.

When I read the story of Hannah, she struck me as a person who entered some degree of depression. What she was experiencing had to have been so real. Her heart was broken, and her life had been affected by it. How could anyone understand her?

Time to Seek the Lord!

Reflecting on my experiences as a servant of God, a husband, and a minister of His word, I have experienced some dark moments. Many times, I thought I was not going to come out of this trial this time!

I have never checked myself for clinical depression or gone to counseling for disappointments, unfulfilled expectations, loneliness, heartbreaks, personal or ministerial failures, unfulfilled promises, or personal character battles. I was taught that every test and trial has a purpose. I am called to find out what is happening in the heavenlies and proceed to walk it out by faith!

Regarding Hannah's battle, one might be tempted to ask: where is God in all of this? God is still on His glorious throne, directing Hannah's destiny. I don't think Jehovah God ever left her side, not for a second.

I still believe God doesn't leave our side to deal with issues of utmost importance. Just like Christ was in the boat asleep during the storm, He is with us amid our storms!

Chapter 4

Dealing with Reproach!

Reproach – disgrace; shame.

Spiritual Reproach – is the unkind opinion or judgment some-one holds against you that, no matter how hard you try, you can't seem to shake.

Carrying the burden of reproach is challenging; however, God can make one stand and put that servant in a place where no one can touch him.

When I ponder Hannah's life, I can never imagine the pain she carried within. Hannah was, without a doubt, a woman of faith and dependence upon God like very few in her day. She would later prove to the world how to overcome spiritual reproach.

I thought about this as I wrote this chapter and kept thinking, no wonder we all get discouraged at the idea of being unpro-ductive. When we don't see the fruit of something we have invested in for so long, it is easy to lend our ear to the voice of the enemy and believe the devil's report of negativity.

Dealing with Imperfection

As believers, we often believe that Christianity is synonymous with perfection. It is one thing to hear a non-Christian criticize a born-again believer and point out all their deficiencies, and altogether a different issue when Christians themselves point out another believer who is not as perfect as they are.

Many believe everything will be perfect if you belong to the Christian faith. Your life, your work, your children, your health, your economic status, your marriage, your child-rearing ability, all of it will be perfect and beyond reproach. I hate to break it to you, but this is not an accurate idea of Christianity.

One may be able to make better choices once one hears the truth in God's Word, but it is not a sure guarantee that the believer will discipline himself to those practices mentioned in the Bible. In other words, they should, but too often, they don't have the discipline to make the changes. The output is a life full of stumbles and falls along life's journey.

Reproach Is Often Inevitable!

There are times in our lives when we go through seasons of duress- seasons so challenging that those watching you from afar will wonder if this trial will break the camel's back. The trial is so severe that they notice your change in attitude; your behavior in your faith begins to wane, and those who once stood with you and by you will separate themselves from you. Go figure.

No one wants to associate with failure; they all want to be part of a success story. This shows us how frail humanity is. I repeat, reproach is often inevitable.

Now, some failure is caused by our own foolishness. At other times, failure is necessary as a form of spiritual pruning in and for our lives. God will see that no matter what kind of failure you face, He will use it for His glory and restore us to His heart.

A Lesson on Pruning

Pruning my garden during the fall is not one of my favorite times of the year. I don't like to see branches and flowers cut off my rose bushes, oleanders, hibiscus plants, or any flowery beds I might have, but the fact remains that it is needed. If no pruning is done, the plant will not grow to the next level of beauty.

Others may think it insane to cut off the pretty branches, especially those with flowers and fruit. People may reproach me for doing it, yet I know why I am doing it and have lived to see its fruit.

I believe God sometimes prunes away with fervency and always knows what He is doing even though we don't. We might get mad at God for it or blame Him for it. However, we will live to see the fruit of His work!

Hannah's Spiritual Reproach

Regarding Hannah and her barrenness, Peninnah ensured she pointed out her defects. She would provoke her, make fun of her severely, and blame her because she was barren.

Let me reiterate spiritual reproach. It is the unkind opinion or judgment someone holds against you that, no matter how hard you try, you can't seem to shake.

You see, Hannah felt there was nothing she could do to change her situation. She had no answers. She would have to face Peninnah daily to hear her words, criticisms, etc. This situation grew worse by the day.

From Peninnah's point of view, Hannah was a disgrace. She

would never let Hannah live her situation down.

I don't know about you, but this story hits home very close. I have felt reproach many times. I have accepted God's care over me throughout the years, but it hasn't been easy. This is the reason these notes are very close to my heart.

I don't know about you, but have you ever had someone look down at you and wag their heads, and without saying anything out loud, you could hear them in your spirit saying, "You poor loser! You will never amount to anything! You won't ever make it! You will never have what it takes! You are so pathetic! No wonder no one likes you or wants you!"

I might be exaggerating, but very little. The enemy has a way of hitting us where it hurts us the most. He knows how we beat ourselves up when we lock ourselves in our rooms and turn off the lights. He watches how we long for a breakthrough, a shot at redemption, restoration, and some of the things we have lost because of our errors. He watches the tears; he hears the prayers but continues to beat us up emotionally.

My dear friend, the Lord knows your situation. He is not far from you that He cannot save. In times of feeling unworthy and feeling that the enemy would blame me for the things I have done, the things I don't have, or the things I will never have, I put my trust entirely in Jesus. He can make me stand!

Chapter 5

Aspirations of a Burning Heart!

"He will baptize you in the Holy Ghost and Fire!" – Matthew 3:11

"Be fearless in the pursuit of what sets your soul on fire."
-Author Unknown

In pursuing the heart of the Lord and studying Hannah's life, I have, for the most part, understood that living out our God-given purpose in life has both aspirations and challenges.

We must all be like good farmers; we must plant and wait until the crop comes! A heart full of God's faith must be our motivation.

Spiritually Pregnant?

My counsel to anyone who is carrying in their spiritual womb the desire to give birth to something God has placed in it is to get ready to face the enduring part of giving birth to it. It won't be easy, but if one dares to believe God has promised, that servant will eventually be rewarded.

It is one thing to aspire to please God in every way possible, to carry out His righteous wishes, and to want to fulfill them; however, life is a little more colorful than that.

You see, every aspiration has its challenges. Every desire will be met with opposing forces and confronted with various adversities.

Too many promises have died because the carrier didn't know the timing of it, the method God would use, or failed to see the hand of God amid harsh adversity.

Consequently, these servants never see God's work done due to a lack of discernment, vision, and overwhelming impatience.

Hannah's Heart

Hannah knew something that no one else knew. She carried within her the desire to have a child. Peninnah knew something was brewing in Hannah's heart but didn't know exactly what it was, apart from the natural desire to have a child.

Now, Hannah's husband had some insight into all of this. He knew Hannah wasn't too happy with being barren. He knew what she wanted, but there was nothing Elkanah could do about it. Just like the people who surround us day in and day out, they are clueless about the matters of a spiritual womb!

It Is Not Her Idea!

I don't believe Hannah was just heartbroken by the fact that she was barren. It almost seems like the need to have a child was stronger than the barrenness. Yes, but why? I believe God instilled that in her spirit-man. Her desire to be pregnant wasn't the same desire that Peninnah had when she was pregnant.

I believe Hannah was coming to a place of giving birth to something way bigger than her and the nation of Israel. It seems that she was about to come in touch with destiny, and her child would play a big part in the transitional and spiritual government of Israel. She didn't know, but she was unsettled, unhappy, and dissatisfied with her present condition of barrenness!

Desires, visions, and aspirations are all well and good. All these things are good qualities to have. Yet, when it comes to God being the Lord of our lives, none matter.

You see, God is interested in what He impregnates you with, not in the stuff you impregnate yourself with. Do you get me?

Hannah is Pregnant with Desire!

The thought of having a child for Hannah was tremendous. It didn't seem like it at first, and perhaps in time, she would come to terms with the awful truth that she was barren, but she didn't! She never accepted the fact. Are you hearing this? She was overtaken with the idea of having a child; you see, it wasn't her idea! It was God's idea.

How Does God Make Things Happen?

If an idea is birthed in the flesh by carnal means, then man is always trying to have meetings on how to make this or that come to pass. Man begins to take his idea and does everything he can to bring it to fruition.

I have heard many sincere servants of God say, "We want to do this project for the glory of God. Will you get behind our plan?" and so on.

Let me say that when God calls a man to do something for them, God will bring in the means to make this idea come to pass. If He gives out a plan, He will bring it to fruition using His methods. Let us look deeper into man's approach to trying to help God bring something to pass:

First, man tries to create concepts and ideas that others have proven and tested, saying, "God gave me a vision to do this!" That servant of God must be honest with himself and say, "I copied this from him or her." If there is something that a man cannot borrow, it is someone else's vision. To do so is to fail from the start.

Secondly, the man or woman of God must understand that the idea wasn't birthed in the flesh; it didn't come by human will. God birthed it in the womb of one of His servants. Trying to keep something going when God is not in it is like putting new upholstery on the Titanic!

Wisdom will teach anyone (who seeks the face of God) that if something is birthed in the heart of God, it must be maintained and kept till its finishing stage by the heart of God.

Lastly, being that it was birthed in the heart of God and placed in the heart of His servant, then it will be by the Spirit of the Lord that this vision will be carried out. God's vessel must trust God with the project and lean wholly on God's knowledge and wisdom to get it done.

Anything less than the Spirit of God's leadership will not work! Listen to the great words from God's servant to China, Hudson

Taylor, when he said, *"Depend on it. God's work done in God's way will never lack God's supply. He is too wise a God to frustrate His purposes for lack of funds, and He can just as easily supply them ahead of time as afterwards, and He much prefers doing so."*

Chapter 6

Have You Ever Settled for Less?

"And whenever the time came for Elkanah to make an offering, he would give portions to Peninnah his wife and to all her sons and daughters. But to Hannah he would give a double portion, for he loved Hannah, although the LORD had closed her womb." (1 Samuel 1:4, 5)

When Receiving a Double Portion Is Not Enough

When is receiving a double portion of anything not a very good thing? When is receiving special attention not a good thing? It is not a good thing when something better is waiting for you! This is precisely what was happening in Hannah's life at this time.

Can you see the awkwardness of this? Elkanah gave Peninnah and her children portions, but to Hannah, since she was barren, he would give her a double portion, for, in all honesty, he felt sorry for his wife, Hannah.

If there is something no human can hide, it is the burning desire to have something or be something in life. Hannah was not looking for just something external; she was looking for that thing that called out from deep within, that precious thing that God had imparted and was now deeply embedded in her!

Are You Guilty of Settling for Less?

In this section, I ask: Are we guilty of settling for less? Did we give up on the promise? Did we stop fighting like madmen to get what we know God has given us? This may be your own story to testify on.

How often have we gone so far as to pursue what we believe was God's will for us, only to quit at the start or halfway through the program, project, or work? Perhaps too many times to count.

Those Things Are Good but Irrelevant to God's Will!

In remembering some things about my life, I have experienced this too many times to deny it.

Most people around you don't know where you are with God. They don't have the slightest idea of what God is doing in you or where God is taking you at specific times. These are just facts.

As I was writing this chapter, I remembered an opportunity that came my way about 35 years ago as I worked as a staff pastor in a midsized church in my region. The invitation was for me to leave my pastoral duties for greener pastures.

A dear pastor brother offered me to leave with him to pastor in another city and help him pastor his church. The offer was great, and it was also very tempting to leave my present ministry for a bigger, more established one. This was a great challenge. Let me tell you why.

You see, my life was barely starting in the ministry, my pay as a pastor was low, and the opportunities to build a more significant ministry would not soon happen at my local church. This man of God had a vision and needed someone to help him develop his work. I would lie if I told you I didn't consider it.

I told this dear brother, " Give me a few weeks to pray and fast. Whatever I hear from the Lord regarding this open door, I'll share it with you." I took my time to seek God and felt the Lord say that I was not to go.

Everything externally seemed limited; things were not *happening* at my pace; of course, things seemed even more inviting to pick up and leave. But God had other plans.

There will always be good suggestions by well-meaning individuals. There will always be greener pastures that surround us. There will also be more excellent opportunities that promise to give us a better life.

Only God Knows Our Hearts!

No one understood Hannah. At first glance, one would say she only wants a child- at least here on Earth, it looks that way. But I have seen how earthly things have a way of growing strangely dim. Most people pursue earthly stuff, but people who relate to God desire to please God in all things.

As I said, many people will surround us with opinions about what God might say. Yet, in their wisest ways, they still don't know what God will do with you.

In Quietness of Spirit

People close to us may know us to some degree; they may know our fears, doubts, etc. Those who know us longer will know more significant details of our lives.

As I studied the Scriptures, I didn't get the sense that Hannah was a strong-willed woman. I don't feel she was a demanding wife or troublemaking gossiper. I don't know; maybe it's just me, but I sensed Hannah as a woman who feared the Lord and had simple desires to be a great wife to her husband and a mother to her children.

When one's nature is not prone to spiritual warfare, fighting for what one wants is difficult when one's life resembles a quiet and gentle spirit. I have noticed that people with this demeanor usually let others go first; they typically hide behind the crowds and would instead let others take first place at any given opportunity or occasion.

When Push Comes to Shove!

I have met many people with this personality; however, when push comes to shove, they turn into someone else. The deep person of the spirit, that individual hiding behind the shadows, comes forth with great authority and confidence. It is truly something to behold!

Hannah was about to wake up and be turned into another person!

Chapter 7

When Push Comes to Shove!

"And her rival also provoked her severely, to make her miserable, because the LORD had closed her womb. So it was, year by year, when she went up to the house of the LORD, that she provoked her; therefore, she wept and did not eat." (1 Samuel 1:6, 7)

Have you ever heard the phrase *when push comes to shove!* Where does this saying come from? What does it mean?

When push comes to shove is often linked to rugby. In this sport, momentum shifts rapidly. Players may start with a gentle nudge against their opponents. But soon, this can turn into harder pushes and aggressive shoves.

The definition means to use one's strength to force oneself through a crowded area.

I believe it was only a matter of time before Hannah's life would be transformed by her circumstances, not to mention the inward battles she was facing.

Hannah quickly began to disintegrate inwardly from what seemed like endless battles with her rival Peninnah. It says that **"year after year, she was provoked severely to make her miserable; therefore, she wept and did not eat."** Can you picture this?

Misunderstood, Patronized, and Starving!

When God allows us to go through a time of wilderness testing, a season of what some call the dark night of the soul, one is not looking for comprehension of the situation; that person is looking for something that will quench the sinking feeling inside them!

I want to show you four elements we will face as we are challenged with deep anguish to see God's will fulfilled in our lives.

Hannah's Shortcomings and Inabilities!

The first challenge comes from our inability. Hannah couldn't help herself as much as she wanted to. She was barren, and nothing would change that, of course, unless God showed His mercy to her.

She looked at herself and knew it. "I can't have children; I can't, I can't, I can't!"

Was she trying to remain positive? Of course, she wasn't. She was devastated at the fact. What would she do, and how would she explain to her friends and family? What would she say to her husband? What a mess!

You and I will face these inabilities. It may not be barrenness like Hannah, but you might face paralyzing fear, overwhelming doubt, or demon powers destroying your self-esteem. How often can one hear, "You are worthless!" until you eventually start believing it?

Peninnah, the Provoker!

The second challenge comes from Peninnah, the provoking voice.

We all have had people in our lives who have provoked us somehow. Some do it on purpose, yet others do it unknowingly. Those who do it purposefully intend to hurt the individual; they do it with a spirit of degradation. Out of their wounded hearts, they provoke and hurt others. I'm sure you have met some like these.

Now, there is another group. These are the ones who provoke you without knowing that they are provoking you to act, to take a risk, or to have faith in some endeavor. When they do this, they don't know anything about your present situation; they unknowingly prophesy to your spirit.

I'm not sure if Peninnah felt left out since Elkanah would give Hannah the double portion or if Peninnah was upset that Hannah would get most of the attention around the house and not her. Whatever the case was, Peninnah was adamant in provoking Hannah with her disgraceful words.

I have always believed that no matter who provokes you, take it as a challenge and follow what is in God's heart for you!

Elkanah, the Voice of Reason!

Then Elkanah, her husband said to her, "Hannah, why do you weep? Why do you not eat? And why is your heart grieved? Am I not better to you than ten sons?" (1 Samuel 1:8)

The third voice will come from our family and friends.

I call this the voice of reason because, in Elkanah's mind, it seems that he didn't understand his wife's pain; he attempted to provide outward substitutes for what Hannah was missing internally.

Many people will come along and share sound reasoning. They will say, *"Maybe it wasn't meant for you."* Or *"Perhaps it is not God's will for you to have, to hold, to share!"* etc.

In Elkanah's case, I believe he had reached a breaking point and confronted his wife about her behavior: **"Hannah, why do you weep? Why do you not eat?"**

These are legitimate questions, but her heart was in too much anguish to try to explain what she was feeling. Then it happened – Elkanah said, **"Am I not better to you than ten sons?"**

Listen to Hannah's reply to her husband – oh wait! There was no reply, only an action. Here is the action: **"Hannah arose after they had finished eating and drinking in Shiloh."**

There is no comment on Elkanah's foolish statement. Did you catch this?

As a wise rule: Never criticize, patronize, or provoke someone who is being dealt with by the Lord!

Eli, the Undiscerning High Priest.

Here is one more element that I find attacking us amid our anguish and fight for our destiny in God.

I value the counsel of the servant of God and have, countless times, made decisions based upon their counsel and experience.

All believers should have someone in their lives to help them along the way. Whether it be a pastor, a cell group leader, a discipleship leader, a spiritual mentor, a true friend in the faith, etc., these vessels of God are indeed a gift from God in the body of Christ. We don't discard the wisdom from the elders!

As valuable as mentors are in our lives, they are not God. God has also given us His Spirit to lead us on the way. We must also train ourselves to hear God's voice and discern the times and seasons God is bringing us into.

Sometimes, no spiritual mentor or pastor will know where we are with God. They will mean well, but they won't know where God is taking us. Sometimes they will, but sometimes they won't! We must know this.

In the case of Hannah and her burden of barrenness, Eli was probably unaware of what was happening in Elkanah's family.

If you don't know something about someone, don't play the role of a prophet; this only hurts people in the long run. They will end up hating you.

A Season of Prayer

Hannah's pain and anguish were genuine to her, so she decided to go to the temple and spend time with God in prayer. **"Now Eli the priest was sitting on the seat by the doorpost of the tabernacle of the LORD. And she was in bitterness of soul and prayed to the LORD and wept in anguish."** (1 Samuel 1:9-10)

When you look at this picture, you will find a lazy, undiscerning high priest sitting on one end, and you will see the broken Hannah in anguish and bitterness of soul at the altar of prayer.

As to Hannah's need, Eli, the High Priest, seems oblivious to Hannah's bitterness of soul.

Drunk In Anguish!

"And it happened, as she continued praying before the LORD, that Eli watched her mouth. Now Hannah spoke in her heart; only her lips moved, but her voice was not heard. Therefore, Eli thought she was drunk. So, Eli said to her, "How long will you be drunk? Put your wine away from you!" (1 Samuel 1:12-14)

As Hannah pressed into God's heart and vowed to the Lord, she spoke in her heart. The Scripture says that only her lips moved, but her voice was not heard. Without her knowing, she had an audience; Eli was watching.

Eli knew nothing of what it meant to pray in bitterness of soul or anguish in the heart; he was clueless.

If I had to take a wild guess, this man didn't know anything about praying in the Spirit. This man had never been to Calvary! He had never died to himself! He had never taken the burden of the Lord seriously!

At the end of this scene, the best thing Eli could determine was that Hannah was drunk! Can you imagine this? Eli said, **"How long will you be a drunk? Put your wine away from you!"**

When it comes to finding alignment for our spiritual lives, when it comes to knowing God's will in greater detail, or when it comes to knowing what season of our lives we are entering – only anguish of soul will get us there!

Chapter 8

Enough Is Enough! Mindset

"So it was, year by year, when she went up to the house of the LORD, that she provoked her; therefore, she wept and did not eat." (1 Samuel 1:7)

"...Year by year..."

By the sound of the narrative, it appeared that Hannah would have to revisit this experience every year. She would have to relive the barrenness, the reproach, the mockery, the patronizing, and the false hopes of ever becoming a mother.

If this wasn't enough, we could also add the loss of appetite and the sleepless nights, probably due to depression and much bitter weeping.

This experience, or set of experiences, set Hannah on a different path she perhaps never intended to walk- the path of brokenness, anguish, and bitterness of soul.

Let me share a powerful truth that will quiet our hearts in God and set us on a path of prayer and power.

Seeing the Invisible!

A big part of walking with God is that the servant of the Lord must learn to live a distinctive life—a life of faith.

If our spiritual walk begins with a life of faith, it must be kept and maintained in God's faith, not man's. When we finish our race, it must also be done in God's faith, not man's.

The error of many believers, at least from what I have seen and learned from my own experience with God, is that we cross over from a spiritual perspective to a natural one.

As believers, we start to claim natural blessings when God didn't promise anything natural, or initially, it had to be birthed in our spirit first, then the natural, in this order.

Tending to the Spiritual First

I'm not saying that God doesn't bless with material things, but the servant who truly walks a broken and contrite life with God is focused on God's eternal purposes.

A servant who has caught a glimpse of what I am speaking of understands that God births things in the spirit first, then the natural. We must tend to the spiritual first!

They don't make false claims that God said this or that. They know all too well that God reveals to the spirit in the innermost being first; after filtering it through the cross, they conclude whether it is God. This is the divine pattern.

When this servant catches a glimpse of God's heart, he will persevere until it comes to pass, whether it be children, finances, a career, a job, or some type of ministry.

True servants that walk in God's revelatory realm only fight for what is God's! They won't waste their time with nonsensical stuff.

Looking for an Earthly Promise!

"After these things the word of the LORD came to Abram in a vision, saying, "Do not be afraid, Abram. I am your shield, your exceedingly great reward." But Abram said, "Lord GOD, what will You give me, seeing I go childless, and the heir of my house is Eliezer of Damascus?" Then Abram said, "Look, You have given me no offspring; indeed one born in my house is my heir!" And behold, the word of the LORD came to him, saying, "This one shall not be your heir, but one who will come from your own body shall be your heir." Then He brought him outside and said, "Look now toward heaven, and count the stars if you are able to number them." And He said to him, "So shall your descendants be." And he believed in the LORD, and He accounted it to him for righteousness." (Genesis 15:1-6)

Taking Father Abraham as our leader and example in the walk of faith, we learn that one of Abraham's battles was waiting upon the Lord for His perfect timing in bringing forth a son for him and his wife, Sarah. As you know, this wasn't easy for Abraham and Sarah; waiting is never easy; it wasn't then, and it isn't now!

While Abram contemplates his future, while his heart is building up a certain type of anguish, the word of the Lord comes to him in a vision— **"I am your shield, your exceedingly great reward."**

This is so like the Lord coming and speaking to us about His nature, His beauty, and His heart towards us; the Lord doesn't even mention Abram's own future or Abram's concern with it.

Was Abram's future important to God? Of course, it was! But there should be no fear when our future is in God's hands! Let us take note of this and learn.

In response, Abram asks the Lord, **"Lord GOD, what will You give me, seeing I go childless, and the heir of my house is Eliezer of Damascus?"** Then Abram said, **"Look, You have given me no offspring; indeed, one born in my house is my heir!"**

If you look closer at this story, Abram insists on discussing his future and heir. Do you see how easily we get sidetracked from God's nature to our nature and selfish needs? How easily do we get moved from the beauty of God to the mundane?

To settle Abram's heart and bring peace to him, the Lord speaks to Abram and says, And behold, the word of the LORD came to him, saying, **"This one shall not be your heir, but one who will come from your own body shall be your heir."**

Refreshed in God!

After hearing God's heart and clarifying his future, the Lord refreshes Abraham's spirit by asking him to step outside. **"Then He brought him outside and said, "Look now toward heaven, and count the stars if you are able to number them." And He said to him, "So shall your descendants be."**

Unless we are willing to step outside and allow God to speak afresh to our anguished hearts and weak faith, we won't regain our spiritual stamina and attain a fresh vision from heaven.

It's not until God gives us this freshness that we can quench the anguish, for we will know in our hearts and minds that everything will be well with us.

No wonder Hannah ran to the altar of prayer; it was the only place to find refuge for her anguish. No wonder Abram stepped outside his tent; it was the only way to calm the anguish. My friends, it will be the same with you and me!

Fresh Vision Comes to Those Who Wait!

"Why do you say, O Jacob,
And speak, O Israel:
"My way is hidden from the LORD,
And my just claim is passed over by my God"?
Have you not known?
Have you not heard?
The everlasting God, the LORD,
The Creator of the ends of the earth,
Neither faints nor is weary.
His understanding is unsearchable.

He gives power to the weak,
And to those who have no might He increases strength.
Even the youths shall faint and be weary,
And the young men shall utterly fall,
But those who wait on the LORD
Shall renew their strength;
They shall mount up with wings like eagles,
They shall run and not be weary,
They shall walk and not faint." (Isaiah 40:27-31)

All spiritual renewals are found in the fountain of waiting upon the Lord in the secret place of prayer. One is renewed in God when one falls prostrated before Him with a broken and contrite heart.

Once the servant of God becomes one [entwined] in mind and heart with God, that dear man or woman of God will soar with new strength, be mounted with wings like an eagle, and run and not be weary and walk and not faint! Bless His holy Name!

Chapter 9

For Out of the Abundance
Of My Complaint and Grief!

"But Hannah answered and said, "No, my lord, I am a woman of sorrowful spirit. I have drunk neither wine nor intoxicating drink but have poured out my soul before the LORD. Do not consider your maidservant a wicked woman, for out of the abundance of my complaint and grief, I have spoken until now." (1 Samuel 1:15, 16)

Hannah's Prophetic Life

Pondering Hannah's life, one can only say that this woman faced some serious adversity. You and I have probably been through some difficulties as well.

I don't believe Hannah's life is just some tear-jerking motivational story in the Bible to build our faith in God. It is more than that. I believe her life story, as depicted in 1 Samuel chapter 1, is a prophetic portrait of someone who longs to live their life to the fullest in God.

I am convinced that this story is a prophetic word for those who long to please the Lord with all their heart! Yes, Hannah's life is not a story of romance and intrigue; no, sir, it is a life of passionately pursuing Christ's heart and mind for every generation that gets to read it.

From the Lips of Hannah!

"No, my lord, I am a woman of sorrowful spirit."

When I read how Hannah made her way to the temple to seek the face of Jehovah God, she had one thing in view: to meet God and get justice!

Hannah was no *drama queen*, and she was not trying to get attention from the high priest either. Hannah could care less what anyone thought of her. I truly believe that if this sincere woman of God were to be interviewed by some local television station and asked why she was making such a big deal with all the praying at the altar, she would quickly answer, **"I am a woman of sorrowful spirit."**

To the body of Christ, I ask, "Do we need more than *a sorrowful spirit* to send us to our face?"

Many have never allowed themselves to be carried by the Spirit of the Lord to the place where God truly wants to bring them to. There are too many reservations, too many theological per-spectives, and yes, too many carnal excuses not to obey the Master!

Pursuing the things of God has never been cheap but costly. It has never been easy but difficult. If one cares to follow God and pay the expensive price to obtain what was promised, one will have to make one's bed in tears. One's life will be a living sacrifice to the Lord day in and day out.

Unless the man or woman of God is captured, empowered, and learns to overcome by the act of God's vision in them, the birthing of it won't take place.

Captured by Vision!

The key to a life full of joy is knowing deep within your spirit that your God-given life was created for so much more. Once you know that God has impregnated you with a picture of the future, deep desires, and persevering passions, the servant of God will begin to make the necessary changes to his or her life to align it with God's wishes.

When someone says, I see something in my spirit; God spoke

to me about this or that. Know that God's vision has captured this person. It is not their words that touch you but how they attempt to rearrange their lifestyle to accommodate God's vision. Anyone can recognize a man or woman on a mission!

My Personal Pursuit of God

In my pursuit of the Lord's heart for my life, when the Spirit of the Lord touched me and baptized me with His desires, my life could no longer be kept inside a box. I longed to be alone with God; I longed to go where people didn't want to go; I yearned for the opportunity to tell others about the saving power of Jesus!

I can truly say that my whole being was moved as if something had transpired, and I was taken captive by God Himself. I no longer wanted my own dreams, plans, and ambitions. All I wanted to pursue was that something that burned deep within.

Empowered by Vision!

Obviously, when someone knows that God has called them to a higher standard of thinking, acting, and living, their lives will move from the natural realm to the supernatural realm. This is also clearly seen in these servants.

They will not be deterred from accomplishing what burns in their hearts. You see, it is not them but God empowering their souls. This is the way of those empowered by God's vision.

Though challenges come, they find strength from God to keep going. Though people may criticize them, they will not give in to such foolish attempts. They know their lives are in God's hands, not man's.

They have one thing in view and only one thing – give birth to God's expression.

Overcomer by Vision!

I believe God has called many servants of God to give birth to His expressions; however, too many of God's servants have settled. The obstacles in their lives, somehow or some way, convinced them that they couldn't or wouldn't get what God promised, and they settled for second best.

Perhaps they were on their way to fulfilling their destiny in the Lord when they entered a season of having one tragic situation after another, and for lack of vision, they opted out of giving birth to God's heart.

They took the bait from the enemy himself and settled for what man could give them or for what they could get using or leaning on their own strength, and not what God had in store had they allowed their anguish to melt at God's altar of prayer!

Nothing makes the devil tremble more than when a man full of anguish can pray to God and pour his heart before God.

Chapter 10

Until the Anguish Leaves!

"So, the woman went her way and ate, and her face was no longer sad." (1 Samuel 1:18)

So, [she] went her way and ate, her countenance no longer sad." (1 Samuel 1:18 Amplified Version)

"...and went her way. Then she ate heartily, her face radiant." (1 Samuel 1:18. *The Message Bible*)

Many have walked this path and could testify of the painful ordeals they had to overcome to find joy. I'm sure many have persevered and lived to tell their stories. For those who have experienced the birthing of a vision, the struggle, you are not alone. As a matter of fact, it is God's way of giving birth to His desires to affect Earth.

If there is something that anguish will do inside everyone who has experienced it, it is this: it will change you! It will bring you and me to our faces! It will challenge our spiritual stamina to the core.

I once heard a man say that adversity separates men from boys and women from girls—I believe it. Unless you are willing to be used by the Lord, you will not pass the testing season. You will not endure such harshness unless you see the Father as the One holding the cup of your pain.

Please understand me; some people end up falling away because of anguish and discouragement. This is a fact. Don't ever get the idea that breakthroughs are automatic. They can be if you have learned to ascend and live in the heavenly places, but they are impossible if you have yet to learn Christ and have never entered the fellowship of His sufferings.

There are casualties in God's army. One must be alert, pray, and fast to gain a breakthrough. Breakthroughs are not always what you think they are; sometimes, they involve coming to terms with God's purpose for your life.

On a different note, there are believers today who have managed to sidestep God's will and embrace a pseudo-will of God. They will vow and say, I really, really love the Lord with all my heart! Of course, they do until all hell breaks loose and the fire of His glory begins to lead them down a path filled with loneliness and anguish.

It is at this level of aloneness that the servant of Christ is truly tested. Here is where real faith is gauged by our patience and perseverance!

A Celestial Breed!

I don't know about you, but the closer I look at Hannah's life, the more I see my own lack of power through prayer.
This Woman Was Unstoppable!

She had caught a glimpse of her future and was fully convinced that what she was seeing in her spirit would come to pass. Hannah did not consider her body just like Abraham did not consider his as he prayed and believed for a son of promise, as it says in Romans 4:19a, **"And being not weak in faith, he considered not his own body now dead...".**

Apparently, Hannah's anguish had catapulted her to the next level of intercession, and she would not be denied her prayers. Hannah was not about to walk away empty-handed!

The sweet Spirit of the Lord reminded me of the story Jesus shared regarding the widow and the unjust judge, listen:

"ALSO [Jesus] **told them a parable to the effect that they**

ought always to pray and not to turn coward (faint, lose heart, and give up). He said, In a certain city there was a judge who neither reverenced and feared God nor respected or considered man. And there was a widow in that city who kept coming to him and saying, Protect and defend and give me justice against my adversary. And for a time he would not; but later he said to himself, Though I have neither reverence or fear for God nor respect or consideration for man, Yet because this widow continues to bother me, I will defend and protect and avenge her, lest she give me intolerable annoyance and wear me out by her continual coming or at the last she come and rail on me or assault me or strangle me. Then the Lord said, Listen to what the unjust judge says! And will not [our just] God defend and protect and avenge His elect (His chosen ones), who cry to Him day and night? Will He defer them and delay help on their behalf? I tell you, He will defend and protect and avenge them speedily. However, when the Son of Man comes, will He find [persistence in] faith on the earth?" (Luke 18:1-8 -Amplified Version)

I don't know about you, but Hannah somehow knew about the principle of getting justice, fervent prayer, and continual coming to God. She was going to bother God until the break-through came until the anguish left her mind and heart. Now, that is determination!

When Hannah prayed at the altar and Eli, the High Priest, watched her, the Lord gave her the breakthrough. It is also interesting to note how signs and wonders accompanied this breakthrough. The sign was that she was now hungry enough to eat; in other words, her appetite returned, and the radiance of God was beaming from her face! To God alone be the glory!

As the Lord moves in you and me, and it seems like victory is never arriving, but we continue praying and fasting, suddenly, the light will break through, and our sadness will be taken away. This is the reward for those who wait upon the Lord for the release of God, for the birthing of His vision.

In closing this writing, if you are facing delays and what was promised is not arriving, if overwhelming anguish has moved into your soul and spirit, not to mention the enemy making his presence known by discouraging your heart, here is what I say, press into the Lord in prayer and fasting! Drink the cup of pain that the Father has prepared for you. Remain steadfast in the faith and allow yourself to be embraced by His loving arms. The time is coming and is very near when the Lord will wipe away every tear!

The LORD bless you and keep you;
The LORD make His face shine upon you,
And be gracious to you;
The LORD lift up His countenance upon you,
And give you peace." ' (Numbers 6:24-26)

Even so, come, Lord Jesus!

My Journey's Lessons